The Unbroken Pastor

Pastor Roland Stroud

DEDICATION

This book is dedicated to every person who is enduring trials and tribulations. Psalm 3:5-6 says, "Trust in the LORD with all thine heart; and lean not unto thine own understanding. In all thy ways acknowledge him, and he shall direct thy paths." In other words, God will take care of you!

May God bless you,

Pastor Roland Stroud

Contents

Introduction

This book has been written to encourage anyone who has experienced or continues to experience life trials and tribulations. I pray that this book encourages you to trust and lean on God because He will always take care of you. Your first step is to acknowledge that the battle is not yours, it's the Lord's. *Isaiah 41:10* (KJV) states *"Fear not, for I am with you; Be not dismayed, for I am your God. I will strengthen you, yes, I will help you, I will uphold you with My righteous right hand."*

May the Lord bless you and keep you. May His face shine upon you and be gracious to you. May He lift up His countenance upon you and give you peace.

Chapter 1

I was born in Macon, Georgia on February 10, 1949. My parents were William Stroud and Addie Kate Jordan. I was born and raised in Unionville, which was a very poor neighborhood. Rose, my twin sister, passed away as an infant because my parents could not afford the proper medical care. I attended Unionville Elementary School located in the Unionville Community. It was an all-black school. Because of segregation it was prohibited for blacks and whites to be educated in the same classrooms. We didn't have many material possessions, but we did have God and He supplied all our needs and some of our wants. *Philippians 4:19* (NKJV) states, *"And my God shall supply all your need according to His riches in glory by Christ Jesus."*

As African Americans, growing up in the South, our diet consisted of foods that were less desirable to people who were more affluent. We enjoyed foods like chitterlings and fatback. My mother worked as a domestic. Some of her duties included cleaning houses and ironing clothes. My father worked at Maxwell Brothers Box Factory in Macon. This was a time when the community truly believed that it took a village to raise a child. It was also a time when neighbors understood the importance of protecting each other, especially the children. They did not believe in sparing the rod. *Proverbs 13:24* (NKJV) states, *"He who spares his rod hates his son, but he who loves him disciplines him promptly."*

Chapter 2

At a young age I was a ladies' man who had a lot of female friends. I was a good student, maintaining a "B" average throughout elementary school. I was also exceptional in math and spelling. At an early age, I joined and attended Center Hill Baptist Church located in Macon. Back then it was an old camp Wheeler House, located on Marigold Avenue. The Pastor was Reverend H.R. Rancifer. He was one of four ministers who was arrested for sitting in the front of the bus. The other three ministers were Reverend Cameron Alexander, Reverend E.S. Evans, and Reverend Van J. Malone. They stood up for their civil rights by refusing to give up their seats.

According to my recollection, it was around the year 1962. During this time there was a saying, "If you were white, you were right but if you were black you had to get back." It was commonplace for black people to be referred to as the "N" word. Even the churches were segregated. I always wondered how people could pretend to serve God when they had so much hate. The Word of God says to love everybody. *1 John 4:20* (KJV) states, *"If a man say, I love God, and hateth his brother, he is a liar: for he that loveth not his brother whom he hath seen, how can he love God who he hath not seen?"*

Not all white people were like that. I fondly remember the late Buck Melton who supported the Bus Boycott. He would come by the mass meetings and leave money so the protestors could buy gas for their cars. Regardless of the situation God always has a ram in the bush. Not only have I seen blacks treated unfairly but, I have also witnessed heinous acts against people of color.

I realized that blacks were second class citizens compared to white people. This was very disturbing because I knew God created us all.

Genesis 1:27 (KJV) states, "*So God created man in his own image, in the image of God created he him; male and female created he them.*" I also realized at an early age that I had fast and quick hands, so I began boxing and I was very good. I was trained by an exceptional boxer named Andrew Fuller. Even though he was skilled he did not have the speed and quickness that I had.

Chapter 3

As a child I remember when a group of friends and I were attacked by a white man for walking in his neighborhood. The police took us to the Juvenile Detention Center. When we appeared in court the judge stated that we were a bad group of boys and should be punished, despite the white man being wrong. This was just some of the things that people of color had to deal with.

I attended Ballard Hudson High School, the same school where the late Julius Adams attended. He went on to play professional football for the New England Patriots. If walking to school wasn't bad enough, we had to endure insults by white students who called us names as they drove by on the school buses. Segregation was everywhere. We could not escape it. From terminal stations to restaurants, you would see signs that read, "whites only." We were living in a time where we were treated so badly. I remember that there was only one police car that would patrol Unionville and it was called "Car 46." The city hired two black police officers, Joe Gaskin, and Walter Jones, but they did not have the authority to arrest white people.

Some of my worse memories include a time when I accompanied my mother to work because I did not have to go to school that day. I vividly remember my mother working so hard, cleaning, cooking, and ironing clothes. That day, everything appeared to be fine until around noon when the man of the house came home. Shortly after arriving he called his wife into the bedroom. When they came out, he immediately left, and she began to act strangely. My mother asked her if there was anything wrong and she said that her husband did not want two black people in his house at the same time. My mother told me to go home because she needed the money. I cried all the way home because I wanted to get him back. But I remember my mother telling me God will take care of it. *Romans 12:19* (NKJV) states, *"Beloved, do not avenge yourselves, but rather give place to wrath; for it is written, "Vengeance is Mine, I will repay," says the Lord."*

Chapter 4

I would eventually begin working. I rode a bicycle delivering groceries after school. I made $15.00 per week, and I would give my mother $5.00 every week. At the age of sixteen, I bought my first car, a 1953 Ford, for $200. During that time, $200 was a lot of money. That car was raggedy, but it did run. My friends and I had a lot of fun in that old car.

During that time, we did not have streetlights, but nobody feared the dark. We were forbidden to go into certain neighborhoods. One place was Tatnall Square Park. One day, we decided that we were going in there. A fight broke out and with the help of God we won the fight. We couldn't lose because God was with us.

I would eventually have a baby girl by Martha, and we named her Kimberly. I had another daughter by Valerie, and we named her Shonda. Then came my first true love,

Rosemary. She was the cousin of Norman Nixon who played for and won two NBA championships with the Los Angeles Lakers. When I met her, she already had a son named Anthony. Rosemary and I were buddies. I helped her raise, Anthony. We were so in love but neither one of us had a relationship with God. We had two more boys, Derrick, and Roland. We were married for twenty-two years before divorcing. The devil caused both of us to do things that really hurt our marriage. 1 *Corinthians 13:4-8* (KJV) states, *"Love is patient, love is kind. It does not envy, it does not boast, it is not proud. It does not dishonor others, it is not self-seeking, it is not easily angered, it keeps no record of wrongs. Love does not delight in evil but rejoices with the truth."*

Chapter 5

I would eventually meet Mae Helen Wilson. We fell in love and got married on August 15, 1992. I joined the Ash Street Church of God in Christ (COGIC) and soon thereafter the Lord called me to become a minister. Bishop C.J. Hicks licensed me as a minister, and I was ordained as an elder in 2002 by Bishop Jack Stephens. Our family suffered a devastating loss when Helen's father was killed. Our grief was further impacted when Helen's son was murdered by his wife. This was a hard struggle to deal with. But God promised us that he would never leave us nor forsake us. So, we trusted in the Lord. *Hebrews 13:5* (NKJV) states, *"Let your conduct be without covetousness; be content with such as you have. For He Himself has said, "I will never leave you nor forsake you."* *Proverbs 3:5-6* (NKJV) states, *"Trust in the Lord with all your heart, And lean not on your own understanding; In all your ways acknowledge Him, And He shall direct your paths."*

Living a happy and healthy life. I worked for the Macon Transit Authority for eleven years before retiring in 2011. In 2001, I was named Employee of the Month and Employee of the Year. I also received the Mayoral Award from Mayor Jack Ellis. In 2007, I met Oprah Winfrey while working as an ambassador for the city of Macon. In that same year, I also met Little Richard Penniman.

My wife's son Robert started the Power of Love Worship Center in 2012. He would later relocate out of the state but not before appointing me Pastor in 2014. I have been Pastoring ever since. Our first location was a storefront Church building, Bentley's Chapel, New Pilgrim Annex Building, 824 Woodard Ave, and we would eventually move to 562 May Avenue, where we are currently located.

Chapter 6

In 2018, I started having health problems that resulted in a loss of blood. To improve my condition, I received one blood transfusion after another. I would also have to have two stents placed in my arteries. I was going from one doctor to another to no avail because they could not determine the cause of the bleeding. Emory University was highly recommended, but they still could not find the cause. I became very tired, but I would not give up despite the severity of my illness. I am a living testimony that all sickness is not unto death. I am reminded of *John 11:4* (NKJV) states, "W*hen Jesus heard that, He said, "This sickness is not unto death, but for the glory of God, that the Son of God may be glorified through it.*" It's not always the tree that's leaning to fall. "What am I saying?" All sickness is not unto death. God can stop you from leaning.

During the process I had forty-two blood transfusions. I was at church one Sunday when I passed out. The ambulance was called, I was placed on the gurney and by the time they rolled me halfway down the aisle, I heard the voice of God telling me to get up. I got off the gurney and went back into the pulpit. I trusted God because He has always had my back.

God sent me an angel who scheduled me an appointment at the Mayo Clinic in Jacksonville, Florida in 2019. To this day, I still don't know who she was. But isn't that just like God, He just doesn't show up, but He also shows out. They clipped and cauterized those arteries and I have not bled since. However, the devil didn't stop there. I had a heart attack, stroke, two more stents, a defibrillator, pacemaker and COVID. I know you are probably wondering how he is still alive. The answer is I favored God and God favored me. I was tired but not scared. I had my house in order, so I was not afraid of death.

Chapter 7

I'm reminded of Hezekiah in the Bible who was sick unto death but because God favored him and he favored God, he was blessed with fifteen more years. I turned to God and confessed that I just recently started living according to your Word. There was a time when I served the devil and just didn't do right. I have not always served you the way I should have. We always use the phrase, "Ain't nobody perfect" when we are looking for an excuse! But *Matthew 5:48* (KJV) states, *"Be ye therefore perfect, even as your Father which is in Heaven is perfect."* Jesus was talking to the disciples. You will never be perfect in the flesh, but you can be perfect in the spirit.

Despite how you feel you must bless the Lord at all times. *Psalm 34:1* (NKJV) states, *"I will bless the LORD at all times; His praise shall continually be in my mouth."* The devil will entice you with temptation. Temptation is an attempt to get someone to do something wrong. His mission is to kill, steal and destroy. *1 Corinthians 10:13* (NKJV) states, *"No temptation has overtaken you except such as is common to man; but God is faithful, who will not allow you to be tempted beyond what you are able, but with the temptation will also make the way of escape, that you may be able to bear it."* *John 10:10* (KJV) states, *"The thief cometh not, but for to steal, and to kill, and to destroy: I am come that they might have life, and that they might have it more abundantly."*

My wife was diagnosed with cancer, but God took care of that too. She is cancer free. Life is unpredictable. You don't know what might happen from day to day. However, when God favors you, it makes a difference. I am encouraging you not to give up. Despite what you are faced with. Give it God and let Him handle it. *Isaiah 40:29-31* (KJV) states, *"He giveth power to the faint; and to them that have no might he increaseth strength. Even the youths shall faint and be weary, and the young men shall utterly fall: But they that wait upon the LORD shall renew their strength; they shall mount up with wings as eagles; they shall run, and not be weary; and they shall walk, and not faint."*

28

Chapter 8

Living without the Lord on your side is not living but merely existing. The whole duty of man is to fear God and keep His commandments. We all have our burdens to bear. *Proverbs 1:7 (NKJV)* states, *"The fear of the Lord is the beginning of knowledge, But fools despise wisdom and instruction."* Psalm 23:4 (NKJV) states, *"Yea, though I walk through the valley of the shadow of death, I will fear no evil; for You are with me; Your rod and Your staff, they comfort me."* There were times when I got tired and was ready to give up, but I thought about the goodness of the Lord and all He had done for me, my soul cried out Hallelujah and I thank God for saving me. *Romans 10:9 (KJV)* states, *"That if thou shalt confess with thy mouth the Lord Jesus, and shalt believe in thine heart that God hath raised him from the dead, thou shalt be saved."* If you are going through a difficult time in life, first examine yourself and see where you are in relation to God.

If you have not repented, go to God, confess your sins, and repent. Remember no resurrection, no salvation. The devil wants you to fail by giving up, but you must trust God. Don't worry about death because we all have an appointment. Death is not the end. *Hebrew 9:27* (KJV) states, *"And as it is appointed unto men once to die, but after this the judgment."*

Chapter 9

Somebody said that God will make a way. Not only will He make a way, but Jesus is the Way, the Truth and the Life. You must be born again. Repent of your sins and live according to God's Word and His Will. You will still have problems, but God will be there for you. *He will never leave you nor forsake you.* He's a doctor in a sick room, a lawyer in a courtroom and a shelter in a storm. Some things may be too big for you, but they are just right for God. There's nothing too hard for Him.

I told you earlier that we came up poor. One day we had nothing in the refrigerator, but my mother told my sister to set the table. We thought she was losing her mind. She left and after a while we saw her coming down the street. She had so many grocery bags she had to holler for us to come and help her. She told us that God works like that. God touched other people's hearts and they gave her all those groceries.

"*Won't that be a time when we get over yonder*." Oh, my Lord, what a time. I am presently seventy-four years old. I've made three scores and ten (at the time of this writing). Sometimes I get weak, but I'm still trusting in God. No, I'm not ready to die but I am prepared. Heaven is a prepared place for prepared people. *Hebrews 11:1* (KJV) states, "*Now faith is the substance of things hoped for, the evidence of things not seen*."

I have salvation which guarantees my deliverance from evil, danger and trouble. This special gift only comes from God. Life is not about what you possess, what kind of car you drive, what kind of house you live in or how much money you have. It's about your relationship with Jesus. He's the best thing that has ever happened to me. Jesus paid the ultimate price so we all could be saved. In this life if you are going through a battle, I want you to know that *the battle is not yours, but God*. I hope this book has encouraged you so you can understand that God loves you. I'm praying that God finds favor in you.

God Bless You!
Pastor Roland Stroud

www.ingramcontent.com/pod-product-compliance
Lightning Source LLC
Chambersburg PA
CBHW020656160726
47991CB00003B/1212